HOW DO ASTRONAUTS WEE IN SPACE?

Dr Dino's Learnatorium

DINO

Published by Dino Books,
an imprint of John Blake Publishing Ltd,
3 Bramber Court, 2 Bramber Road,
London W14 9PB, England

www.johnblakebooks.com

www.facebook.com/johnblakebooks
twitter.com/jblakebooks

This edition published in 2015

ISBN: 978 1 78418 653 1

British Library Cataloguing-in-Publication Data:

A catalogue record for this book is available from the British Library.

Design by www.envydesign.co.uk

Printed in Great Britain by CPI Group (UK) Ltd

1 3 5 7 9 10 8 6 4 2

Papers used by John Blake Publishing are natural, recyclable products made
from wood grown in sustainable forests. The manufacturing processes conform
to the environmental regulations of the country of origin.

Every attempt has been made to contact the relevant copyright-holders, but some
were unobtainable. We would be grateful if the appropriate people could contact us.

Introduction

The universe is an amazing place. As a scientist, I can't think of anything more exciting than exploring outer space to see what mysterious wonders are out there. Also, as the last surviving dinosaur on Earth, I live in the hope of being the one who makes the discovery I've waited my whole life for: finding a planet ruled by non-extinct dinosaurs! I know it's out there somewhere ...

But all those humans out there who aren't scientists and astronomers (people who study outer space) might wonder what is so important and interesting about space. Sure, it might be cool to see a UFO sometime, or be abducted by aliens, but what are the chances of that actually happening?

Trust me: even though it seems pretty boring and empty, outer space is just about the most fascinating, remarkable and outright crazy place you'll ever hear about. You've probably heard that every star out there is actually a sun – but have your teachers told you that when a star dies it explodes with such force that it destroys everything in its solar system in an instant and can create a black hole? Or that there are so many stars out there that it would be impossible to count them all? In fact, right now we think there are about 100,000,000,000,000,000,000,000 stars out there, which is more than every grain of sand on Earth!

Your teachers have almost certainly made you memorise dull facts like all the names of the planets in our solar system, and even taught you a silly little phrase to force you to remember in which order they come. But when you complain about the weather, have they told you that on Jupiter a storm has been raging for over 300 years, and that it's more than three times the size of Earth? Or that it gets so windy on Neptune that they've clocked gales going faster than the speed of sound at 1,500 miles per hour?

And I'm sure that your teachers will have spoken to you about the Moon and how it orbits the Earth every twenty-eight days; maybe they even mentioned that its gravity causes high and low tides here on our planet. But have they told you that the Moon was probably formed when another *planet* crashed into Earth and smashed a big chunk off it? Or that Moon dust is everywhere on the Moon and it causes space hay fever (which is incredibly annoying for snotty astronauts in spacesuits who can't wipe their noses)?

So there's a lot more to space than the black sky you see at night, even if your teachers don't want you to know about it! Here in my learnatorium, though, you can learn about all of these incredible facts and much, much more. And who knows? Once you've learned everything I've got to teach you, maybe you can get your own telescope and help me to find my dinosaur-infested planet – and then help me to build a dinosaur-friendly spaceship so I can get there without tearing it to pieces!

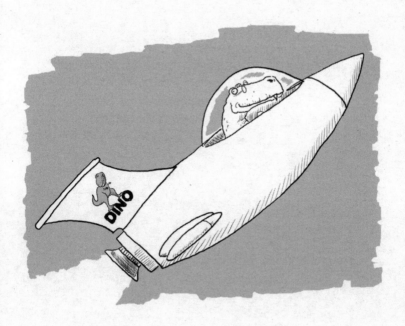

What Is Space?

Before you start trying to learn from me everything that my learnatorium can teach you about space, it's important to understand what space actually is. Your teachers will probably tell you that it is called space because that's exactly what it is: empty space. But, as is usually the case with teachers, they are only half-right.

Outer space is what scientists like me call a vacuum, which means that it has absolutely no matter in it – not even the tiniest little bit. Matter is what we are constantly surrounded by on Earth. It is everything from the ground we walk on to the water we drink and the air we breathe. Matter literally makes up everything on Earth that has mass and takes up room. In space, though, there obviously isn't any ground or liquid and, what's more, there are no gases at all, which is why humans (and dinosaurs) couldn't last long out there. There's simply nothing for us to breathe.

However, that doesn't mean that space is completely empty. In fact, it's teeming with activity ... we just can't see it.

Dr Dino's Simple Introduction to Space

How cold is space?

It depends on how close it is to the Sun – or any other star that gives off lots of heat – but temperatures in deep space are the coldest possible in the universe: -270.45°C. Not even penguins could survive at that temperature!

Put your scarf on if you're going to play out there.

What colour is space?

Not black. The black you think you see is actually the absence of any light and therefore is not really a colour. Space is actually a mixture of all sorts of colours, from green and blue to purple and turquoise – it's just that it's hard to see them from Earth.

What does space sound like?

Nothing. Sound cannot travel through a vacuum, so space is completely silent.

Does the fact that astronauts are weightless mean that there is no gravity in space?

Even though objects float around in space, there is a lot of gravity out there. For example, gravity is what causes galaxies to form and the Earth to orbit the Sun.

How long could a human (or dinosaur) survive in space?

It's hard to be exactly sure ... because, surprisingly, nobody has volunteered to be the test dummy for this experiment! And I wouldn't suggest you be the first.

Fortunately, you wouldn't suddenly explode or freeze in an instant like they show you in some Hollywood movies, but it's expected that you would lose consciousness after fifteen seconds and die after about two minutes. The basic answer is: not long. So don't try it.

So, if there's no matter in space, what is there?

That's quite a confusing question, and human scientists argue about it all the time, but quite simply, it's an awful lot. Everything from light rays to heat rays, from interstellar dust to solar wind, from *galactic cosmic rays* to *solar energetic particles* (tricky terms to remember, but it will impress your friends if you can) and other forms of radiation. Most of these things are incredibly powerful and dangerous, and would kill a human pretty quickly if they were out in space for too long, even with a spacesuit.

So, if your teacher ever tries to tell you that space is a vast, empty place ... tell them to get their facts straight.

How Big Is Big?

What's the biggest thing you can think of? Whatever it is, multiply it by 1,000 and then another 1,000. Even then, I can guarantee that it won't be as vast as our universe. You see, however hard humans try to think about how big the universe is, they can't. It's literally *unimaginable* how massive it is (to humans at least. Dinosaurs can imagine it just fine. I think it must be because our brains are so much bigger). But here's a good way to try to understand it.

You are just one small animal on a very big Earth. Compared to me, all humans are tiny, but let's take the tallest person ever as an example. His name was Robert Wadlow, and he was an impressive 8 feet 11 inches tall. There would have had to be a chain of 14,733,500 Robert Wadlows lying end-to-end to reach all the way around the world.

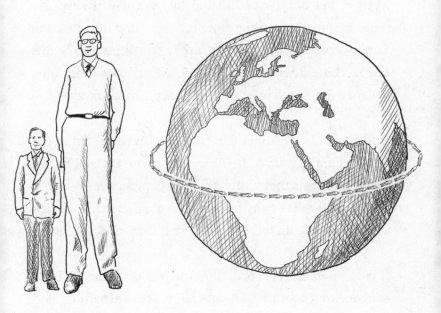

If you find it hard to imagine so many Robert Wadlows, here's something I do in my learnatorium, which you can do in your garden to help you put our solar system in perspective. Let's make that massive chain of Robert Wadlows – the Earth – the size of a football. If that was the case then, by comparison, the Moon would be the size of a tennis ball, and the distance between the tennis ball (Moon) and the football (Earth) would be just over 7 metres.

Maybe that doesn't sound too far, but if you keep the same comparisons, then how far away do you think the Sun is from our football-Earth? If you want to try this out in the garden then you had better have a big one, because the Sun would be just under 2 miles away!

And what about Alpha Centauri, the nearest star to the Earth? That's 93,000,000 miles away from the real Earth, and that means that in our game of perspectives it would be 480,000 miles away from our football-Earth ... which is further away than the real Moon is from the real Earth!

If you've managed to follow all of that then you're halfway to becoming an official space learnatour, and you probably know more than your teachers already. But the solar system, big as it is, is only one *teeny tiny* part of our universe. In fact, just in our galaxy, the Milky Way, there are 300,000,000,000 other stars – and a lot of them are way bigger than our Sun! If you imagine the Earth being as big as a grain of salt, then the Milky Way would still be 5,100,000 miles wide.

The Milky Way might seem big, but compared to the universe it's still pretty minuscule. That's because it's one of just 100,000,000,000 galaxies that humans can detect

with current telescope technology … and that's a number that will probably rise to nearer 200,000,000,000 when you humans make telescopes as good as the ones in my learnatorium.

So when we talk about exploring space, what we really mean is exploring the insignificant part of space we can get to. There's so much out there that not even my learnatorium – or my enormous brain – can cope with it. And do you want to know the scariest part?

The universe is still expanding – at roughly 46 miles every second! Good luck ever reaching the end …

The Man in the Moon

Ever since you humans figured out how to fly – which dinosaurs were doing literally hundreds of millions of years before you – people have looked up at the Moon and deep into space, and wondered if they would ever get there. The answer, of course, was yes. But the journey into orbit was a wild one.

Eleventh Time Lucky

NASA's spaceship *Apollo 11* was the first manned mission to land on the Moon and you probably know who was on board: Neil Armstrong and Buzz Aldrin, the first humans to walk on the Moon. But there's a lot that your teachers probably haven't told you. Here are my three favourite facts about it from my learnatorium:

1. Americans are very proud of the fact that Armstrong and Aldrin planted an American flag on the Moon, which they think will be there forever. Actually, when they took off to leave the Moon, the exhaust blew the flag right away.

2. Armstrong might be the man who took the first step on the Moon, but Aldrin was the first one to wee on the Moon! And he did it with an audience of around 600 million people watching him!

3. Although Neil Armstrong famously said: 'One small step for man, one giant leap for mankind,' he actually had to take a 4-foot leap just to get on to the Moon, which for you puny humans is a pretty huge step.

And finally, spare a thought for poor Michael Collins. 'Who?' I hear you ask. Well, he was the third member of *Apollo 11*, but he had to stay back with the ship while the other two got all the glory, which is why you've never heard of him!

As a Tyrannosaurus rex, I only have short arms – something I've always been quite embarrassed about. However, my short arms are a real advantage in one way: they get me out of playing golf, which must be the

most boring and pointless sport ever invented. Alan Shepard must disagree, though, because he flew all the way to the Moon with a golf club and two balls, and in 1971 hit two shots from the Moon's surface.

Not only did he become the first person to play sport on the Moon, but because of the low gravity there, they may well be the two longest golf shots ever hit.

Apart from two golf balls, humans have left a number of things on the Moon over the years, following a visit. For example, there is a miniature statue of an astronaut up there, alongside a list of all the astronauts who died trying to explore space.

However, far more interesting – and disgusting – than that is the fact that humans have left behind about ninety-six bags of wee and poo since their first trip there because scientists wanted to 'lighten the load' on the spaceship for the trip back to Earth. What's really gross is that those same scientists now want to bring the poo back to examine it! They think that all the bacteria living off it might have mutated into something new and alien because of all of the space radiation to which they were exposed.

So just imagine ... the first aliens we come across might feed off human poo!

I still dream of being the first dinosaur to set foot on the Moon (my assistant learnatours have almost finished my rocket ship), and when I get there, I will be the thirteenth earthling to make that giant leap. NASA have sent twelve American astronauts to the Moon so far on their *Apollo* missions but, incredibly, nobody has been there since 1972 – that's over forty years ago.

Farting is always funny. That's a fact. But on the *Apollo* missions, passing gas was no laughing matter. In fact, the NASA scientists were so worried about it that they did two whole studies on what happened when you farted in space.

Why were they so concerned? Because when humans let one go, they release large amounts of hydrogen and methane (although nowhere near as much as dinosaurs do ... trust me!), and both of these gases are flammable. NASA thought that if the astronauts farted too much, this could cause a huge explosion on the spaceship! Fortunately, that never happened ...

All the same, they realised pretty quickly that when you're in a spacesuit, there's nowhere for that smell to go.

Since there are no parents up there to do the house-work (actually – as a scientist I have to be accurate – it's because there's no wind or water), the Moon is a very dusty place. What's worse, that dust isn't like what we have on Earth: it is space dust. It's sharp and jagged, and smells like gunpowder. After spending a few hours on the Moon, the astronauts reported that it gave them space hay fever, made breathing difficult and even ate through their space boots, pretty much destroying them! In fact, the dust is so bad that we scientists think it will be the biggest problem for future human (and dinosaur) settlers.

Will humans ever go back to the Moon? The simple answer is: yes. NASA already have detailed plans to send astronauts back there, and there are even plans to start building outposts and have up to six humans living there for short periods of time. It might not be too long until

17

the Moon is seen as just another country 'on' Earth. And we won't stop there … scientists hope to have humans living on Mars by the 2030s!

Universal History

If you look up at the sky tonight, you'll be able to see the Moon, the stars, perhaps some nearby planets and, if you're very lucky, a shooting star – which is actually the unscientific name for a small meteor burning up when it enters the Earth's atmosphere. And, because you're clever, you'll know exactly what you are looking at. But what if nobody had ever told you that stars were really far away suns? What would you think they were? And what about everything else you could see?

Well, before scientists like me figured it all out, humans believed some pretty funny things ...

The Milky Way isn't just a tasty little chocolate treat (far too little for me – and there's not enough meat for my taste either); it's also the name of the galaxy of stars where our solar system is. It's made up of hundreds of

billions of stars, and we now know that most of the ones you see in the sky are part of it.

Many ancient civilizations believed ridiculous stories about how the stars came to be in the sky. Some thought that they were the gods' spilled milk, a silvery river to heaven, scattered cornmeal or even part of an enormous dolphin floating somewhere in space. Not even the silliest dinosaur would have believed any of those.

My favourite myth about the stars (because it's based on science) was thought up by the Finnish people. They call the Milky Way 'The Pathway of Birds' because they noticed that when birds migrated, to somewhere where they believed the 'bird home' was, they followed the line of the stars to the south. Of course, stars have nothing to do with birds, but scientists have shown that birds *do* actually use the Milky Way to navigate their way home!

Whether it's made of cheese or not, the Moon has always been thought to have a strange effect on people. For thousands of years humans have told stories about normal people becoming insanely murderous under the influence of the full moon and vile beasts roaming the Earth waiting to attack. Even today the idea of a werewolf running loose in my learnatorium is enough to send a shiver down my rather sizeable spine ...

In the eighteenth century, they took this one step too far, though. They passed a law in England which meant that if you murdered someone during a full moon, you could plead that it made you insane and there was a chance you might get away with it!

Dr Dino's Demanding Deities

Before the universe was understood, almost all societies believed that the Sun was a god who had the power to give and take life on a whim. Sacrifices, both of animals and humans, were commonplace all over the world as a way to try to appease the Sun god and to get his favour for things like growing crops or starting a family.

Dinosaurs would never be barbaric or unscientific enough to sacrifice each other to some imaginary Sun god! We just eat each other for dinner instead.

Many astronomers thousands of years ago thought that the universe rested on the back of giant animals or gods. It's not just ancient people who had funny views on the universe, though.

There's a story of a famous astronomer who gave a lecture recently, during which he talked all about the universe. At the end an old lady came up to him and said, 'You're talking rubbish. The Earth is a flat plate sitting on the back of a giant turtle.' The astronomer laughed and asked her what the turtle was standing on, if that was the case? She replied, 'Don't try to confuse me, young man. It's turtles all the way down!'

During the Renaissance (from the fourteenth to the eighteenth century), it was believed that the Earth was the centre of the universe, and the Sun, the Moon, the stars and everything else up there revolved around it.

A clever fellow called Copernicus came up with the theory that the Earth revolved around the Sun, and an even cleverer fellow, Galileo, proved that that was the case. Unfortunately for him, not many people believed him at the time. In fact, his views were so unpopular that he was thrown in jail for the rest of his life by the Church for committing heresy!

The Native Americans thought that the Moon was the mother of the stars and would come out at night to dance with her children. They didn't think so highly of the Sun,

however … they believed that he was the stars' father and, when he woke up hungry every morning, he gobbled up his children for breakfast.

Astronewts

In 1783, two Frenchmen took a sheep, a duck and a rooster, put them in a basket and sent them flying up into the air to test their new invention: the hot-air balloon. Why they chose a sheep, a duck and a rooster, nobody will ever know ... but a new tradition had begun – that of humans launching animals up into the stratosphere to see what would happen. And you'll be happy to hear that the sheep, the duck and the rooster all made it home safe and sound.

Oi! There's nothing about this bit in the contract!

Over the years, humans have sent all sorts of living beings out of Earth's atmosphere. The list is too long to write here but it includes: mice, flies, monkeys, dogs, cats, turtles, rats, frogs, geckos, fish, oysters, newts, jellyfish and insects of all sorts, such as beetles, moths and bees. But still no dinosaurs! The reasons for these trips vary from wanting to see if they could survive a trip to space to, basically, just wanting to observe what would happen. All of them have been hailed as heroes, and here are a few of their stories.

The first animals in space were two brave fruit flies, who were fired into space in 1947 on board a captured Nazi V-2 rocket. They travelled a mere 68 miles into the sky and, fortunately for the flies, they made it safely back to Earth after being parachuted down. It's doubtful whether they were aware of their incredible place in the history of earthlings ...

Is that your tummy rumbling, or mine?

The first monkey in space, Albert II, wasn't quite as lucky (although he was definitely more fortunate than Albert I, whose rocket ship exploded as it was ascending). Albert II's mission to get into space was a success, but the parachute deployment was less of one, and Albert II tragically died on impact. Incidentally, Albert III and Albert IV also died inside their rockets ... it wasn't a good time to be called Albert.

Space Dogs

During the Cold War, the Soviets and the Americans were competing in the Space Race, which was the quest to see who could get to the Moon first. The Americans won that one in the end, but the Russians were still very proud of their famous Space Dogs, who broke a number of records and, interestingly, were all female. This was because of the way their spacesuits were designed... if a male dog had gone for a wee in one of those suits, it would have got messy in the spaceship very quickly!

Water bears, or tardigrades as we scientists like to call them, are tiny little animals about half a millimetre long. While their size might not be impressive, their toughness is. In fact, they can claim to be the toughest animals on the planet because when a 2007 mission took them into space, it was proved that they could survive in the vacuum of outer space for TEN DAYS without dying. Humans can barely make it to ten seconds.

Laika is most likely the best known of the Russian Space Dogs. In 1957 she was blasted off into space and became the first living being to survive while orbiting the Earth – a remarkable feat. I'm sure she wasn't too pleased with what came next, though. The scientists hadn't quite worked out at that point how to get out of orbit, so she was doomed, and died several hours after becoming the most famous dog in the world. The Soviets kept that last bit to themselves until 2002, however. I suppose they were a bit embarrassed … but that didn't help poor Laika.

In 2014 a Russian satellite was sent into orbit with five geckos in it – one male and four females – in order to study exactly how they mated in zero gravity, which is a weird and disgusting thing to want to study, if you ask me! Unfortunately, the Russians lost control of the satellite and when the geckos were found, they had sadly perished.

Ham was a chimpanzee (you would think he should have been a pig with a name like that ...) who will be remembered as the chimp that paved the way for the first human to be sent into space. After he survived in orbit while weightless for a number of minutes, NASA decided it was safe for humans, and only three months later the first American was up there. Ham was rescued and lived out the rest of his life in style as a special guest of Washington Zoo.

Spiders have been sent into space a number of times so that scientists could study whether they can still spin webs when they are weightless – which they can indeed do. Even more impressive, though, was the jumping spider Nefertiti, who captures her prey by leaping onto their backs. Remarkably, she could do that even while floating through the air. I was glad to hear that because it bodes well for my own hunting style in space!

In 2003 the space shuttle *Columbia* tragically broke up in the air, killing everyone on board. But not everything. When searching the wreckage, rescuers found that a number of roundworms that had been on board had somehow managed to survive the explosion and the impact! That's almost as tough as a tardigrade.

The first animals to return alive from orbit were, in 1960, a pair of dogs: Belka and Strelka. They became heroes in Russia and Strelka even formed a celebrity couple with another Space Dog. They had puppies, one of which – Pushinka, which means Fluffy in Russian – was given to American President John F. Kennedy as a gift for his daughter. For a while the Americans were concerned the puppy might be a Russian spy ... but they gave her the benefit of the doubt, and it eventually settled down in the White House and had four puppies of its own.

Is There Anybody Else Out There?

Are we alone? Well, I'm alone, but that's because I'm a dinosaur, and sadly the last of my kind. But are humans alone? That's a question people have asked themselves for thousands of years, and the idea of 'aliens' coming to Earth is as old as the Ancient Egyptians and their pyramids.

Nowadays, we imagine anyone claiming to have seen an alien to be a conspiracy theorist who wears a tinfoil hat and has watched a little too much TV for their own good. However, just because there isn't any good, solid scientific evidence of aliens visiting Earth (and there isn't – although I'll come back to alien sightings in a later chapter), it doesn't mean that aliens don't actually exist. In fact, as a scientist with a degree in universal knowledge, I would have to say that it's extremely likely somebody else is out there.

What Are the Chances?

Up until the twentieth century, scientists believed that the Earth was a very special place. Without going into the sort of boring detail that your teachers would love to tell you about and put you to sleep, they used to compare the chances of life developing anywhere else as about as likely as a hurricane sweeping through a rubbish dump and building a jumbo jet. Never going to happen, right?

Well, it's not quite as simple as that. Many events have changed our minds; for example, they believed that for life to exist as we know it, a planet has to be the perfect distance away from its sun. Too close and any life will get fried in an instant; too far away and you would freeze to death faster than a caveman during the Ice Age. That is certainly true, but those scientists believed that the chances of another Earth-size planet forming in the right place would be minuscule. Now, with better telescopes, we estimate that around one in five stars will have a planet like that.

Do you remember how many stars we said were in the universe? Just in our galaxy alone that means there could be as many as 80 billion planets, all capable of life.

So, scientifically, it's really not a case of: 'Are there aliens out there?'
It's really: 'How *many* aliens are there?' Wow!

Life on Mars?

Unfortunately for those of you hoping that some friendly aliens on the next planet might pop over, I can assure you that there are no furry little Martians running around on Mars. On first look it's a barren place, rocky and completely deserted – probably quite lonely for the probes that NASA have sent up to wander around on its surface.

However, much higher methane levels than expected (meaning it smells a lot more like your lavatory than scientists thought it would ...) indicate that at one point in its history there definitely could have been life on Mars! So who knows what the first man (or woman or dinosaur) on Mars might find ...

Can We Contact Them?

Since scientists are so sure that aliens are all around us, why don't we pick up the phone and give them a call? Well, it turns out that some clever people called SETI (the search for extraterrestrial intelligence) have been listening to space for decades in the hope of hearing an alien trying to get in touch with Earth.

At SETI, they constantly have their ears to the sky, listening out for radio waves that can travel incredibly quickly through space and might carry a message to us here from aliens.

Wow! Signal!

SETI haven't had much luck in hearing from alien life forms just yet … except for one exciting occasion in 1977 when Jerry Ehman was manning the Big Ear radio telescope.

For seventy-two seconds, Jerry picked up a radio signal that looked exactly like what we would expect an alien call to look like. He was so thrilled that he wrote an enormous 'Wow!' on the signal, which gave it its name.

Unfortunately, scientists don't always get it right (well, some don't. I always do) and because of the way it was built, Jerry couldn't move the telescope to follow the signal.

Since then, hundreds of other people have searched for the phantom signal in the area of space it came from, but without any luck. One thing we are pretty sure about, though, is that whatever the Wow! signal was, it wasn't natural. It was almost certainly man- − or should I say alien- − made.

Should We Contact Them?

Right now, scientists could be deciding the fate of the world. There is a serious debate going on about whether or not humans should send messages out into space to try to attract the attention of any passing aliens that might be flying by.

The arguments are simple, and I'll let you decide which side you're on. One group argues that if aliens heard us, they would probably be just as excited by us as we are by them, and would want to share information, knowledge and inventions with us. They could help solve all sorts of problems in the world, from hunger and disease to pollution and climate change.

The other group has a very simple argument, which boils down to this: what happens if they don't like us and want to kill us? If they've mastered space travel, the chances are they have the technology to destroy Earth, should they wish to.

So the question is: is it worth the risk? Whichever way you vote, it's worth bearing in mind that NASA have predicted that we will make some sort of contact with aliens by around 2040 ... so we don't have too long to decide what we want to do!

Satellite TV

Isn't it a great feeling to get home from a hard day at school, collapse on the sofa while your parents cook you dinner and veg out in front of the TV? Well, next time you switch on your favourite show, think about this: for decades now humans have been beaming satellite television into space, where it bounces back off satellites towards your home.

However, some of that data keeps on going and is off into the great void of space, where it could be intercepted by anyone … or anything.

So next time you're watching the football with your friends, just have a think about what else might be watching it with you!

The Big Beginning

What created the universe? It's a question as old as … well, the universe. We scientists now have a pretty good idea of what started it all: a huge explosion which we call the Big Bang Theory. And it was a very, very big bang.

Humans only figured that out in the last few decades, so what did people think started it all before that? You probably know that Christians believe that God created the world in six days. But here are my five favourite bizarre creation stories that I bet your teacher never told you about.

5. The Maori of New Zealand tell the story of two giant parents, Rangi and Papa (Papa, believe it or not, being the mum), who lived together in the sky, permanently hugging in a sweaty, sticky embrace. Their sons all lived in between their disgusting skin folds and, understandably, didn't like being in such a dark, smelly

place so they all banded together and forced their parents apart. Rangi flew upwards and formed the sky, while Papa fell and became the Earth. Now they spend their days crying and sighing in sadness, which explains everything like the rain, storms and mist.

4. P'an Ku was a Chinese giant who grew up in a massive egg that contained the entire universe. Finally, after 18,000 years, he decided he'd had enough of waiting around and burst out of it, sending bits flying everywhere, which created the sky and the Earth. Unfortunately for P'an Ku, the effort of breaking free from the egg was too much and his body literally fell

to pieces. His eyes became the Sun and the Moon, his bones the mountains, and his blood the rivers and oceans. And all the little bacteria that lived on him became humans!

44

3. According to the Australian aborigines, the Earth was cold and dark, and the only thing alive was a rainbow-coloured snake that lived deep underground. This snake had a bit of a dodgy tummy and one day he felt like he was going to throw up … so he raced up to the surface and spewed out everything that had been bubbling away inside of him. And that included all the animals and plants on Earth!

Dr Dino's Enormous Explosion

About 13,798,000,000 years ago, the entire universe was bubbling away in a tiny space that was way hotter than the Sun and way denser than your teachers. All of a sudden, the whole mass exploded out so fast that we can't even calculate how quick it was – but it was definitely faster than the speed of light, which is the fastest thing in our universe now.

Within seconds the universe was enormous, bigger than you can imagine, and the explosion was so huge that even now the universe is still expanding from that original bang.

2. The Zunis are a Native American tribe with a bizarre belief: they thought that in the beginning humans were slimy creatures that lived in the dark, and had horns and tails – but no mouths or bums! The Sun-god Awonawilona took pity on them and gave them light to see and mouths to eat. But pretty soon the people were

full-up and noticed a little problem ... they couldn't poo! Luckily for them, Awonawilona also spotted this issue and sorted it out before their stomachs could get too full. And while he was at it, he cut off their horns and tails. What a nice fella.

1. Scandinavians have to deal with some extremely cold weather, so it's not surprising that they believed the world was once just a big land of ice. It's what happened

next that's really weird, though. They believed that a fiery volcano formed and started melting the ice, which dripped and somehow formed a giant cow, as well as an ice giant.

Next, they believed that the ice giant got sweaty and more giants were formed by the sweat from its armpit! These giants were nursed with milk from the cow, who also created more giants herself by licking a massive block of salt. The giants grew up and had children, who eventually killed their grandfather – the first giant – and formed the Earth out of his skin, the seas from his blood and trees from his hair. Finally, the remaining giants somehow turned some of the trees into humans ...

And if you believe any of that, you'll believe anything! Everyone knows it was the Great Stegadon in the Sky who created the first dinosaurs millions of years ago, right?

Why Does Space Smell Like Raspberries?

They say space is such a big place that almost anything and everything is possible. And although we don't yet know if there's a planet full of talking dogs, a world where everything is made of ice cream or an intergalactic war between Jedis and the Empire (all of which, I have to say as a scientist, is extremely unlikely and probably not true), there are a ton of bizarre things out there that we do know about. Here are just a handful of them, but they are my top ten.

10. Black holes – these are some of the most frightening and powerful things in the whole universe, so it's a good thing it's not possible to see them. Formed when stars implode in on themselves, black holes are the densest things in existence. The biggest ones, which are called supermassive black holes, are about the same size as a small star, but are billions of times heavier. Even the

smallest ones, which are about the same size as a city, weigh as much as our Sun.

Because of their extreme mass, their gravitational pull is so huge that they suck in anything unlucky enough to be in the near vicinity, including light, which is why they are called black holes – no light can escape, so they are completely black. To give you an idea of just how powerful these things are, imagine this: if a star gets too close to one of them, it is torn apart in an instant.

9. The richest planet – as a dinosaur, I've never understood why you humans love diamonds. I suppose your inferior small brains are just attracted to sparkly objects ... but

if diamonds are your thing then you want to head to 55 Cancri e, which is only 40 light years away. It might take a while to get there, but it will be worth the wait because the planet is twice as big as Earth, and it appears that one-third of it is made of diamond!

8. Gamma ray bursts – you might think that black holes are pretty scary, but only if you're stupid enough to get too close, right? Wrong. Since the Big Bang, the next biggest explosions in the universe that humanity has come across are gamma ray bursts, which come from deep within black holes.

Gamma ray bursts are enormous blasts of energy and radiation which wipe out everything in their path. And they have quite a big path ... scientists estimate that any planet within 5,000 light years (a very large distance) would be blasted so powerfully that any life would be wiped out. It's even happened on Earth before, about 450 million years ago, during an event that we scientists call The Great Dying. No prizes for guessing what happened to life on Earth then ...

7. Large Quasar Group – our galaxy is huge, around 100,000 light years across. However, the Milky Way

has nothing on the Large Quasar Group, which is the largest structure in the known universe. This group of stars measures a ridiculous 4 billion light years across, meaning that if you jumped onto a spaceship travelling at the speed of light, it would take you 4 billion years to get from one end to the other.

6. Icy heat – Gliese 436 b is covered in ice, so your teacher would probably tell you that it's a freezing planet. However, the temperature there averages a boiling 800°F! The gravity on the planet is so strong that it pulls in all of

the water vapour and forces it to become a solid, so you are left with the hottest ice in the universe. One thing's for sure: a snowball fight on Gliese would turn deadly very quickly.

5. Magnetars – neutron stars aren't that big, only around 12 miles across, but they have a mass greater than the Sun. If you could take a bit of the star (say about the size of a sugar cube), it would weigh more than 100 million tons! Some of these stars spin very quickly and, because of that, they have very strong magnetic fields – and we aren't talking about the sort of magnet that is a little difficult to pull off nearby metal. We are talking about a magnet that obliterates all life within 1,000 miles.

What's more, these magnetars occasionally send out their own gamma ray bursts, which are luckily a lot weaker than a black hole's. Unfortunately, these come around a lot more frequently. In fact, the Earth gets hit by one almost every decade – and it's only a matter of time before a big one comes our way!

4. Intergalactic raspberries – in the centre of the Milky Way there is a huge dust cloud that is made up of trillions of litres of ethyl formate, better known as raspberry

juice to you and me. As I'm a meat-eater, I actually hate raspberries, but I've heard that you humans find them inexplicably delicious.

If you did ever get a chance to visit, I would be wary of drinking too much, though, because in amongst all that tasty juice is a fair bit of cyanide – one of the most deadly poisons to humans there is.

3. White holes – as we've seen, a black hole is something so dense that nothing can escape. White holes are the opposite: nothing can reach their centre and they are constantly shooting mass out.

The only problem with white holes is that, although scientists like me think they have to exist, nobody has ever seen one. And a big white hole in the sky should be pretty easy to spot! However, there is one very good (and bizarre!) theory that could explain them …

The Big Bang that started our universe could have been the explosion of a single white hole, and every time another one explodes, it creates a completely separate universe to ours!

2. Dark matter – teachers can't always be trusted to tell you the whole story, and they will almost certainly have lied to you at some point about matter. They will have told you that the stars, the planets, the meteors and asteroids

… all of that is what makes up the matter in the universe, and there's nothing else. In fact, that is only about 20 per cent of all of the mass in the universe. There's another 80 per cent called dark matter that we know absolutely nothing about.

Scientists know that it has to be there – because of the way gravity works – but nobody can see it, touch it, smell it or interact with it in any way. You could be surrounded by dark matter right now (you probably are!) but there is simply no way of knowing. Even I, with a PhD in Universal Knowledge, couldn't tell you the secret behind the mystery of dark matter.

1. The end of the universe – the more you think about it, the more your head hurts. We know that the universe is constantly getting bigger, but if that's the case then what is it expanding into? I'm not sure any human will ever know the answer to that question.

Any scientist worth his or her salt will have their own theory about what's out there, but there is one thing most of us agree on: a frightening phenomenon called Dark Flow. After the Big Bang, everything in the universe was blasted outwards and has been speeding off into the distance ever since. Except for one area of the night sky …

A little while ago, scientists saw that a whole series of galaxies were being dragged off in the same direction by some 'dark flow'. The only force that can pull enormous objects like that is gravity, and to create that much gravity you would need something truly ENORMOUS – bigger by far than anything in our universe.

So what could be out there? The answer is probably another universe, just as big as the one we live in, bumping up against ours!

Astounding Astronomers

It has taken humans a long time to figure out how the universe works. The great velocirapt-astronomer Windsaur the Wise had already discovered pretty much everything Stephen Hawking has figured out in the last fifty years, and that was 73 million years ago! Just another example of why dinosaurs are better than humans.

Over the last few thousand years, humans have thought all sorts of ridiculous things, from the Earth being flat or the Earth being the centre of the universe to the idea that stars were little holes in a glass ball that surrounded the Earth. But humans have finally caught up with Windsaur the Wise, and it's mainly thanks to these astronomers.

Aristarchus the Mathematician was an ancient Greek and, in about 250 BC, the first human to calculate that the Sun was the centre of the solar system. Unfortunately, the Greeks all preferred to listen to Aristotle – who said that the Earth was at the centre – and it wasn't until nearly 2,000 years later that people finally believed poor Aristarchus!

Eratosthenes was born in 276 BC and about forty years later became head librarian at Alexandria. Normally, I would say that librarians are even more boring than teachers, but the Alexandrian library was pretty special – almost as good as the one in my learnatorium. Eratosthenes knew that the Earth was round and, using the Sun, he measured how big it was for the first time.

Never trust a map he has drawn, though. His map-making skills were worse than mine, and my claws are too big to hold a pencil.

Ptolemy also lived in Alexandria and was born in AD 90. Even though he is known as one of the greatest astronomers ever, there's one big problem with his work – it's all wrong! He worked extensively on the idea that the Earth was the centre of the universe, and he was believed for about 1,500 years! Thanks, Ptolemy ...

One thing Ptolemy did do right was save the work of **Hipparchus** in what was handily called the Handy Tables. Hipparchus was probably the best of the ancient Greek astronomers and he discovered all sorts of useful things, including the distance from the Earth to the Moon, how to measure the brightness of stars and even that the Earth is always wobbling. In my opinion he was almost as wise as Windsaur.

Squeaky Lockyer

Sir Norman Lockyer was born in 1836 and although he was certainly a famous astronomer, his discoveries were more important a bit closer to home. In fact, he single-handedly changed birthday parties for children around the world. While looking at the Sun, he discovered helium for the first time, which in turn led to the all-important discovery of hilarious squeaky voices.

Born in 1473, **Nicolaus Copernicus** finally managed to destroy Ptolemy's idiotic version of our solar system by proving that the Earth did actually revolve around the Sun (although he didn't give Aristarchus the credit he truly deserved).

As he was saying that the Earth wasn't the centre of the universe, which Christians believed, Copernicus was really terrified of how the Church would view his theory. So he dedicated it to the Pope in the hope that he wouldn't get sent to jail or executed (being a great scientist is a dangerous business ...). He needn't have bothered – he died anyway right after his work was published!

Tycho Brahe was a great astronomer but a terrible dueller. He was so bad that he had a metallic nose because his own had been cut off! Nose or no nose, in the sixteenth century he created an incredibly detailed map of the stars and was the first to figure out what a supernova was: a giant star exploding.

Brahe's assistant was a young man called **Johannes Kepler** and the former was always afraid of being outdone by him … with good reason. Kepler came up with excellent laws of motion that described how planets move and he figured out that the Moon affects tides. What's more, after a bad case of smallpox as a child, he was left with terrible eyesight, so in his spare time he worked out how glasses work.

Appalling Astrologers

Astrologers are people who 'read' the stars in the sky and use that reading to 'predict' the future. Their predictions often appear in newspapers and magazines as horoscopes, and many humans think that this is science.

IT ISN'T! And it is very annoying for real scientists like me.

The idea of astrology has been around for thousands of years but even centuries ago, when humans still thought the Earth was the centre of the universe, nobody really believed in it. It's only gullible humans (it's probable your teachers fall into this category ...) who think that someone can look at the position of the stars and tell others what will happen to them that day.

Galileo Galilei, besides having a brilliant name, was a brilliant astronomer. He drastically improved a new invention – the telescope – and was the first person to use it properly to explore the universe. With it he discovered craters on the Moon, rings around Saturn and moons around Jupiter, and he was probably the first person to start to realise how truly massive the Milky Way was.

However, he was also seen as Copernicus's biggest fan and, unlike Copernicus, he didn't die when the Church became angry at him for saying that the Earth wasn't the centre of the universe. In 1633 this great human being was put on trial and held under house arrest for the rest of his life by the Church – all for being cleverer than them!

Even after astronomers realised that there was more to our universe than our own solar system, they still didn't understand much about what else was out there. **William Herschel** built his own telescopes and with their help, he became the first human to appreciate that the solar system itself was moving, along with many other discoveries.

One of the greatest geniuses to have ever lived (at least among the human race, that is), **Albert Einstein** changed the way in which scientists view the universe. His General Theory of Relativity, which he published in 1915, is very complicated, but it showed how space and time can be bent by forces like gravity. This means, among other things, that the faster you go, the slower time goes.

To give you an idea of how weird this is, imagine this: if you could travel around Earth on a spaceship at the speed of light for one year, when you landed again you would find that twenty-two years had passed for everyone on Earth. Weird, right? Almost as weird as Einstein's crazy hair ...

HOW DO ASTRONAUTS WEE IN SPACE?

Nerdy Newton

I'm sure that at some point you will have been told the story of how Isaac Newton was sitting under a tree when an apple fell on his head, knocked some sense into him, and he suddenly understood the laws of gravity.

This never happened, but he did come up with a number of important laws of science which told scientists how gravity and motion work, both on Earth and in space. And he could have come up with a whole lot more if it wasn't for Diamond. No, he didn't get distracted by sparkly rocks like the rest of you humans … Diamond was his dog, who knocked over a candle in his lab and destroyed twenty years' worth of notes!

That's why I have a strict 'no animals' policy in my learnatorium. Except for humans – they are allowed.

He was only twenty-four when, in 1923, **Edwin Hubble** proved to the scientific world that there is more to space than the Milky Way. Before that, astronomers believed that the Milky Way was the entire universe but finally there was evidence that it was really much, much bigger.

But that was only the beginning. He also discovered that all of those new galaxies were moving away from the Milky Way, which showed that the universe was still getting bigger and bigger every second.

Frank Drake hasn't discovered anything magnificent, but he gets a special mention for starting SETI (the search for extraterrestrial intelligence) and coming up with the Drake equation. This is an equation that predicts how many other civilizations there are in our galaxy with whom we could communicate right now. Based on the data we have at the moment, the equation tells us that there are probably around 1,000 worlds out there populated by aliens we could talk to!

Penzias and Wilson worked together in the 1960s to discover the CMB – the Cosmic Microwave Background Radiation (which has nothing to do with heating up your leftover meal from the day before). This confusing-sounding term refers to the background radiation that is constantly floating around in deep space, where previously scientists didn't think there would be anything.

Penzias and Wilson not only discovered this, but they also proved that it was a result of the original Big Bang. The Bang was so big that even now, billions of years later, this radiation is still left over! Thanks to this simple discovery, even those scientists who didn't believe in the Big Bang had to admit that there could be no doubt about it.

Hoyle's Big Bang

Fred Hoyle was an astronomer who had some pretty good ideas but made one really big mistake: he didn't believe in the Big Bang Theory. Before it had even been given a name, Hoyle appeared on BBC radio and mocked anyone who did believe in it, claiming that it was just a 'Big Bang'. The name stuck, and the Big Bang's fiercest critic became the person who gave it its name!

Stephen Hawking is the most famous living astronomer, and he would be welcome at my learnatorium any time, as he is one of the few humans as clever* as I am. He is known for his work on black holes and how they exist, as well as for examining the

very start (and end) of the universe. Incredibly, he has achieved so much while being confined to a wheelchair, and he has the most distinctive voice in the world and, perhaps, the entire universe.

*Well … almost as clever.

Unidentified Flying Idiots

For thousands of years, there have been reports of strange objects in the sky that some humans have taken to calling UFOs, or Unidentified Flying Objects. Despite the fact that almost all of these 'alien sightings' have been dismissed by science as completely and utterly untrue, there are still a huge number of human beings who believe that aliens have visited Earth and abducted people on a regular basis.

Quite why humans think that aliens would travel for light years to get to Earth just to beam someone up and 'probe' them when they could talk to the most intelligent being on the planet – myself – is beyond me. However, this chapter takes a look at just a few of the many 'alien encounters' ... and why they shouldn't be believed. But who knows, I've never been wrong before ... but I suppose there has to be a first time for everything!

The search for aliens has been going on for millennia, and it's even been said by people falsely claiming to be historians that Alexander the Great won an important battle with the help of 'two flying shields' – something ufologists (humans who believe in UFOs) take to mean aliens.

Unfortunately, Quintus Curtius Rufus, a classical historian who wrote about these flying shields, meant *literally* flying shields, and they were actually used against Alexander's forces. The defenders of Tyre, which Alexander was attacking, heated up their shields, filled them with boiling hot poo and then chucked them off the city walls at the attackers.

Definitely disgusting ... but nothing to do with aliens.

The most famous of all UFO tales dates from 1947 and is set in Roswell, New Mexico, which is very close to a classified military base – an area that has become known as Area 51:

One day, a farmer found a whole jumble of mysterious metallic parts in his field, which looked as though they had just fallen from the sky.

Within minutes of calling the sheriff, dozens of military vehicles arrived and whisked away all trace of the wreckage, and shortly after a press conference was held in which it was claimed that it had simply been a weather balloon that had crash-landed. It wasn't until thirty years later that people started questioning the official version of events, and fairly soon conspiracy theorists everywhere smelled a rat. There were many reports of human-like figures being dragged from the scene and they said the original wreckage definitely wasn't a weather balloon ...

Since then, the US government have tried their hardest to pretend that nothing unusual happened there, but witnesses say otherwise. In 1995 a video was leaked, showing an alien autopsy! What more proof do you need? The story is real!

The facts: unfortunately, the story isn't real and, as a scientist and dinosaur, it's my job to tell you why.

1. The weather balloon story wasn't real, and the US government were lying. But that's because what actually crashed was a top-secret atomic bomb detector that the Americans were using against the Russians.

2. The 'human-like' aliens were most likely crash-test dummies, just like those used in cars.

3. The alien autopsy was a fake – even the person who filmed it admitted it.

So, unfortunately, there were no aliens in Roswell, just dummies – both crash-test dummies and gullible dummies who believed in UFOs!

War of the Worlds

In 1938, a radio adaptation of HG Wells's *War of the Worlds* was aired on national radio in America. The book is about a deadly invasion of Earth by Martians, and the show was presented as a series of news bulletins. Unfortunately, many of the people listening had missed the warning about it being fictional and thought that the world was ending! The radio play reportedly caused panicked riots across America.

Many humans have claimed to have seen UFOs, and some of them are fairly important people. In fact, two Presidents of the United States, Reagan and Carter, both declared to have spotted an alien spaceship before serving time in the White House.

Captain William Schaffner was an American Air Force pilot who went on a mission in 1970 to track an unidentified object moving on radar across the coast of England. Contact was almost immediately lost, and his plane was later found intact on the bottom of the North Sea. Schaffner himself was never found. More than twenty years later, a transcript of what were supposedly his last words was leaked. In it, shortly before disappearing, he described seeing an alien spacecraft – blue and shaped like a football.

However, the truth is actually very boring ... the 'unidentified object' was just another plane in a training exercise, and Schaffner accidentally flew his plane into the sea. Whoops! And the conversation? Faked by enthusiastic ufologists.

Creepy Crop Circles

Crop circles are patterns of flattened plants that appear in crop fields, usually overnight, and are supposedly made by landing alien spaceships. In the 1970s and 1980s, thousands of crop circles appeared in southern England and caused many gullible human beings to think that aliens were visiting the country on a regular basis. (Other reasons were also put forward, including psychic farmers and mad, trampling hedgehogs ... aliens actually seem like a sane alternative compared to those!)

However, in 1991 two pranksters came forward, claiming that they were behind the alien phenomenon. They created a crop circle in front of a number of witnesses and then called in an 'expert', who quickly declared it to be a miraculous crop circle created by aliens. In fact, it had been made with nothing more than a plank of wood, a rope and a baseball cap!

Dinosaurs never fell for crop circles when we ruled the Earth, mainly because we never bothered growing crops! Why have a tiny bite of corn when you could have a nice, juicy whole cow?

In Levelland, Texas, one night in November 1957 is sure to have lived long in the memories of people. Over the course of the evening, the local sheriff received fifteen separate calls from motorists reporting that they had come across a 100-foot-long ball of blue light that travelled up the road and caused their cars to stop as it passed overhead.

Ufologists were immediately intrigued because for once there was a significant number of independent witnesses (rather than one crazy alien nutter like there normally is …). However, after only a few hours of investigation, the Air Force decided that it had most likely been an extreme incident of ball lightning, which is almost as amazing as UFOs and, even better, it's scientifically proven!

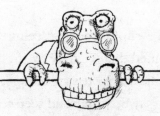

The Skeptic

Michael Shermer is my kind of scientist. He founded the Skeptic Society, which works to attack pseudoscience – like UFOs and astrology – and expose it for being so fake. He produced a TV show where he got young children just like you to make their own 'UFOs' out of things around the house, hang them on a fishing line and take photos of them.

Not only did he trick gullible adults into believing they were real, he even got a photography expert to say that they were just as good, if not better, than many famous 'real' UFO photos!

The first 'modern' UFO sighting was made in June 1947 by pilot Kenneth Arnold, and it's one of the best. He was flying around Mount Rainier when he saw nine shiny objects, all in a row, travelling at what he estimated to be 1,200 miles per hour – faster than any man-made object at the time.

When he landed, Arnold reported seeing 'flying saucers' in the sky – and coined that term for the first time. Although people initially dismissed it as a mirage, other witnesses came forward to say that they had seen something similar ... and soon the story caught the world's attention.

There has never been a proper scientific explanation as to what happened that day, but everything, from clouds of snow to seagulls and from mirages to meteors, has been put forward to explain what Arnold saw. Ultimately, we may never know ...

Thick Theories

There are almost definitely aliens out there some-where, but it seems daft to imagine that they would travel billions of miles just to float around in the sky for a bit and then fly off again. However, there are many worse theories than that about aliens. Here are my top three:

3. The ancient Egyptian pyramids were built by

aliens. The reasons why humans believe this are varied, but it all comes down to the idea that there is a myth that scientists are baffled about how they were built 4,000 years ago and so they must have been built by 'lost alien technology'.

The problem with this theory is that scientists like me know exactly how all of the pyramids were built, which pretty much ruins the conspiracy nuts' arguments.

2. In 1970, two Soviet scientists put forward the theory that the Moon was actually a hollowed-out ancient alien spaceship. Although we know that the Moon isn't hollow, because of the effect its gravity has on our tides (and astronauts have landed on the Moon and it definitely ISN'T a spaceship), a surprising number of humans still believe it.

1. The reptilian theory was made popular by David Icke, an ex-BBC sports reporter who claims to have uncovered a worldwide conspiracy ... that heads of state around the world – including the entire Royal Family and all of the presidents of the United States –

are actually shape-shifting, blood-drinking evil lizards.

Despite the fact that there is zero scientific evidence for this, millions of humans believe it. Apart from being incorrect, it's also incredibly offensive to me and my dinosaur ancestors. If reptiles really did rule the world then, in my opinion, our planet would be a much better place.

Space Men

When humans are in space for long periods of time, their bodies are put in a unique situation that they haven't evolved to deal with: zero gravity. One strange knock-on effect of this alters the human spine. On Earth, gravity weighs you down and compresses the spine, but in space your body can really stretch out, with the result that astronauts can 'grow' up to 3 inches while they are away!

Unfortunately, after a couple of months of being back home, they shrink back down again.

It's not just an astronaut's body that has to re-adjust to gravity when they come back to Earth, though, but their mind as well. Many say that their arms and legs were difficult to control for the first couple of days, but worse than that, almost all astronauts constantly forget that when you let go of something on Earth, it crashes to the floor!

Some advice: never celebrate someone coming back safely from space with your best china.

The International Space Station

Launched in 1998, the ISS is a global project that is effectively a massive laboratory in the sky – something I dream about! Six humans live there at once for months at a time and conduct scientific research on how space affects people, animals, plants and machinery.

It is powered by huge solar panels, which make it the second brightest object in the night sky after the Moon. You can even see it on a clear night without needing a telescope. Try it! But you'll have to be quick. It orbits at the incredible speed of 5 miles per second, so if you blink you'll miss it.

If you ever find yourself floating in space without a protective spacesuit then don't hold your breath. If you did, the sudden change in pressure would cause your lungs to explode.

Moon dust might smell like gunpowder, but have you ever wondered what space smells like? Well, our solar system contains a number of particles of hydrocarbon which smell like metal and diesel. Astronauts, after a long spacewalk, have compared it to burned steak on a barbecue. Incidentally, that's one of my favourite smells.

How Long Can a Spaceman Be a Spaceman in Space For?

Valeri Polyakov, a Russian who was aboard the *Mir* space station for 437 days in one go in 1995, holds the record for the longest period any human has remained in space. This heroic person proved that such a long time in space didn't cause any long-term damage to the human body, and so opened the door for future trips to far-flung planets like Mars.

You humans have very scrawny legs in my opinion (although surprisingly long arms ...) and in space the problem gets even worse. On Earth gravity forces most of the fluid in your body to gather low in your legs, but in space the weightlessness means that it spreads out all through your body, giving astronauts puffy faces and what NASA calls 'chicken legs'!

Sleeping somewhere new is always difficult, but astronauts have a really tough time of it. Not only do they have to be strapped into special beds on the walls (to stop cabin-floating while asleep), but they have also reported seeing flashing lights whenever they close their eyes. Scientists quickly worked out that they weren't going mad, but they were suffering from the effects of cosmic radiation that constantly flies through space. Every time a particle hits their eyelids, it's like a firework going off right in front of their eyes – not great for getting a quick nap!

In any spaceship, the last thing an astronaut wants are things floating around, getting in their way. Liquid is especially dangerous, because if it floats into the machinery then it can cause it to malfunction ... and then anything can happen!

Showers, therefore, are strictly forbidden. And while that might sound like a dream come true, six months spent with five other people and no showers can lead to a very smelly working environment!

There is some good news, though. Weightlessness apparently cures even the worst snorer of their condition, so when astronauts finally get to sleep, it is sometimes their best sleep ever.

Space Firsts

Yuri Gagarin became the most famous man on Earth when in 1961 he was the first human to enter outer space – a pretty frightening proposition considering that nobody really knew if it was safe out there. Sadly, only seven years later, Yuri died during a routine training flight, possibly when his plane hit a bird … perhaps it's safer up in space, where there is no wildlife to worry about!

The first woman in space followed only two years later, when Valentina Tereshkova, a former factory worker, blasted off into orbit. While Yuri only managed less than two hours in space, Valentina was there for almost three full days.

When the first astronauts took off, space food was fairly primitive. Since the last thing scientists want are crumbs clogging up the delicate machinery, all of the food came in tubes, a bit like toothpaste. Now that humans spend so much more time in space, scientists have worked hard to find ways to make their food more delicious and nowadays, just by adding water, astronauts can enjoy everything from tea and orange juice to a full meal of lamb and vegetables. This is important, because there is no way a growing dinosaur like me could survive by just munching toothpaste ...

Almost every astronaut suffers from the same horrible affliction: space motion sickness. For the first two or three days in weightless conditions, it appears that the human body just doesn't know what to make of what's going on. As on a rollercoaster or a ship at sea, the motion sickness can make you nauseous and disorientated, but astronauts have also reported experiencing the feeling of being upside down (which, to be fair, they might have been), as though they didn't know where their arms and legs were.

The real danger here is that throwing up in a spacesuit is obviously really unpleasant ... but it can also be fatal! There's only a limited amount of room in a space helmet and if you can't take it off – because you are strapped into your seat, for example – then there's a real danger that you could choke to death on your own vomit. A truly horrible way to go!

So if you are easily motion sick, perhaps the life of an astronaut isn't the one for you.

The Garn Scale

In 1985 future American Senator Jake Garn was an astronaut who felt sick in space ... really sick. Although NASA have never said how unwell he was, Garn suffered so badly that they now use the Garn Scale to measure how ill an astronaut really is. A full Garn is someone who is 'the maximum level of space sickness ... totally sick and totally incompetent'. Most astronauts never even reach one-tenth of a Garn.

If *everything* floats in space then the big question is: how do astronauts go to the loo? Well, the answer involves these things called 'relief tubes', which aren't completely dissimilar to your Hoover at home ... although shaped in a much more forgiving way. They use suction to suck everything away before it can become a real floater and make things very unpleasant for the astronauts. In fact, this skill is seen as so important that part of every astronaut's training is to perfect this by using a toilet with a camera in it so that they can see exactly what they are doing!

Now, that is all well and good for when an astronaut is in their spaceship, but what about when they are on a spacewalk or strapped in to their seats? For that NASA designed a Maximum Absorbency Garment – or adult diaper – which can hold up to two litres of wee and poo! There are no records as to how often they have been used …

Before humans arrived on the International Space Station, there were already other 'passengers' on board … they weren't aliens, or even dinosaurs, but microbes. These tiny creatures are with us at all times, and mostly they are harmless. However, in the bizarre conditions of zero gravity, they multiply incredibly quickly, and before too long the whole spaceship is covered in mould. So, unfortunately, a lot of an astronaut's time is spent cleaning … it would be like having to clean your room to perfection every single day! Who would want to do that?

Space Disasters

Space is a scary place. No matter how excited astronauts are to be leaving the Earth's atmosphere, they all know that they might never come back. But did you know that only three humans (and no dinosaurs) have ever died in outer space? Three Russian astronauts on *Soyuz 11* died just as their capsule was about to return to Earth when a valve was accidentally opened and the atmosphere on board leaked out into space, causing them to suffocate.

The real danger in space travel actually lies both on the way up and on the way back down. In explosions that shocked the world, NASA's Space Shuttle *Challenger* and Space Shuttle *Colombia* disintegrated during their launch and landing respectively, killing all seven on board in both cases.

As described earlier, NASA were concerned during the *Apollo* missions about the build-up of fart gases in astronauts, which could potentially cause a very smelly explosion. But explosive farts aren't the only thing future space-goers might need to worry about. Richard Branson's team of scientists working on his Virgin space tourism project have suggested that anyone with breast implants might not be able to deal with the change in pressure upon entering space – and the implants might pop right open!

So after reading all of this, do you fancy applying to NASA to become one of the next generation of astronauts? If you do, you should be warned that they have a few requirements. You will need a degree in one of these subjects: biology, physics, maths or engineering. You'll also need to have had at least 1,000 hours of experience piloting a jet plane and you'll be required to pass a NASA physical.

What's more, if you're too tall then there's no point in even trying. Astronauts have to be between 5 feet 2 inches and 6 feet 3 inches. Anything else and you don't stand a chance, I'm afraid.

If you think that's harsh, imagine how I feel! I'm 38 feet 9 inches, so I have a real job ahead of me convincing them to let me onboard.

The Solar Neighbourhood

What's so special about the place 9 billion miles from Earth? That marks the edge of our solar system – the point where the Sun stops being the dominant influence in space. But could humans ever send anything that far? Incredibly, they already have! *Voyager 1* was launched in 1977 and is travelling at 38,000 miles per hour.

In August 2012, the probe passed out of our solar system and became the first man-made object to reach interstellar space. Although I don't often praise humans too much, this was an incredible achievement by the human race!

You may have grown up being told by your teachers that there were nine planets in our solar system, only for them to change their minds and suddenly say that there were only eight. For once, this wasn't your teachers' fault. When Pluto was first discovered, astronomers became slightly too excited and immediately named it as the ninth planet. Unfortunately, that only lasted about seventy-five years and poor Pluto is now only a dwarf planet, along with four other dwarf planets in our solar system.

And here's something that will make Pluto feel even worse about its dwarf status … in January 2015, two new giant planets – bigger than Earth – were possibly found orbiting right on the edge of our solar system. Scientists are still checking whether they are really there or not, which is harder than you would think given they are literally the size of planets! So pretty soon Pluto could fall even further down the solar system's pecking order.

Did you know that part of Mars is right here on Earth? Some meteorites that have landed on our planet have been found to have come from Mars. These rocks were probably knocked off the Red Planet by an enormous asteroid hitting it at some point.

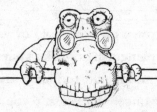

Mighty Meteors and Aggressive Asteroids

Meteors and asteroids are small (well, small compared to planets) bits of rock that travel around our solar system. Scientists think that studying them may hold the key to all sorts of mysteries of the universe, from how life began to how planets are formed.

More importantly, though, is to keep searching the night sky to make sure that nothing too large is coming our way. Although it's very painful for me to talk about, it was quite possibly an enormous asteroid that caused the downfall of the greatest animals to ever live on Earth – the dinosaurs – 65 million years ago. In 2028, for example, a 1-mile-wide asteroid is expected to just miss the Earth. That might not sound like anything to worry about, but if it did hit Earth, it would almost certainly destroy life as we know it and possibly cause human extinction!

Jupiter is a frightening planet – it has hurricanes twice as massive as those experienced on Earth, lightning bolts one hundred times more powerful than anything witnessed on Earth and winds of up to 400 miles per hour. But that is nothing compared to Jupiter's enormous ocean of liquid hydrogen, which is 25,000 miles deep. That's three times deeper than the Earth is wide!

HOW DO ASTRONAUTS WEE IN SPACE?

Your teacher will probably tell you that nothing can survive inside the Sun ... but you had better hope that they are wrong! The Sun's outer atmosphere extends over the Earth, so the entire planet is technically inside the Sun!

What's Next?

As a dinosaur, I can't afford to wait for NASA to build a spaceship that I can fit in – which is why I'm having one built for me in my learnatorium by my assistant learnatours – but maybe they soon won't be the only option for humans trying to get to space ...

Virgin Galactic was founded in 2004 by Richard Branson with the goal of becoming the leading company in space tourism – which to be honest wasn't too hard, because it was pretty much the only space tourism company at that point!

Branson's plan was to develop space shuttles that would take anyone with the money to pay for it into space, and he hoped to get there by 2009. Unfortunately, Branson's team of scientists have found out that rocket science is as difficult as ... well, rocket science, and they still haven't managed to send anyone to space just yet.

Nevertheless, in just a few years you could find yourself queuing up to head into orbit just as easily as you do to jump in a plane now. But you had better get your parents to pay for it ... the tickets are currently priced at $250,000, which might take a big chunk out of your pocket money!

First stop: Moon. Next stop: Mars! Although there isn't an exact date for it yet, NASA have predicted that the first human being will step on to the Red Planet by 2030 at the latest, and possibly even earlier than that.

Mars One – A One-Way Ticket

When NASA finally get to Mars, they will probably find that they aren't the first ones there. And not because Dr Dino has made it there first. Mars One is currently selecting a crew of six astronauts to blast off to Mars by 2026! Is this the opportunity of a lifetime? Maybe – but it had better be, because there's no coming back. Mars One is a one-way mission. When they arrive, the astronauts will set up huts and try to be the first humans ever to live – and almost certainly die – on another planet.

The ESA (European Space Agency) got one up on NASA in 2015 when they landed a probe on a nearby asteroid, which seems very impressive ... until you hear NASA's plans. The Asteroid Redirect Mission is a scheme to take an asteroid, or at least part of one, and transport it through space, before putting it in orbit around the Moon. Then astronauts could study it at leisure, looking for signs of life, precious new minerals and clues as to how the universe began.

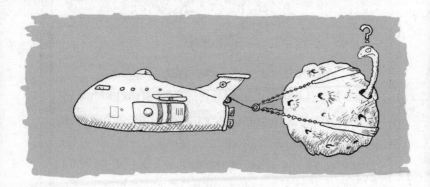

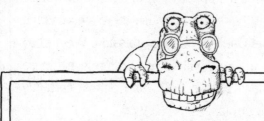

Warp Speed

Travelling faster than the speed of light is incredibly easy – if you happen to be in a science-fiction film. In real life, however, scientists have no idea how anything in the universe could do that ... which is a real problem for space travel! Even the nearest star to the Earth (apart from the Sun) is over four light years away. And if you're thinking that four years isn't too long a time to get to a whole other solar system, you would be right, because the fastest spaceship humans have ever built would take a mere 19,000 years to travel that distance!

And if humans ever do manage to build a spaceship that could travel at the speed of light, just make sure you aren't on it. Travelling at that speed would cause all the hydrogen in the air around you to become powerful blasts of radiation that would kill you instantly. So for the time being, until we figure out something pretty special, space travel will be limited to our own solar system.

Don't worry, though. I have the learnatorium working night and day to sort this one out.

Over the next fifty years, space, and how we view it, will change an astronomical amount. While today only very,

very few humans – and even fewer dinosaurs – have ever left the Earth's atmosphere, by 2065 it is predicted that millions will have visited space, and quite possibly thousands will be living there in colonies on the Moon and Mars.

What's more, we will probably have had our first contact with aliens and who knows what else we will find in the vast expanse of space. It was only a little over one hundred years ago that humans learned how to fly (dinosaurs figured that trick out hundreds of millions of

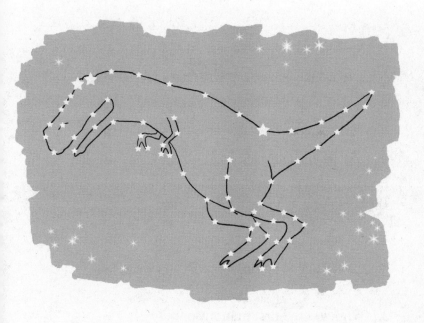

years ago … but I won't rub that in). It's incredible how far the human race has come in that time, and even more incredible to think of where it is going!

Quiz

1. How long ago was the Big Bang?
   A. 120,000,000 years ago; B. Half an hour ago;
   C. 13,798,000,000 years ago;
   D. 400,000,000,000,000,003 years ago.

2. Who was the first man in space?
   A. Neil Armstrong; B. Yuri Gagarin; C. Alexander
   the Great; D. Winston Churchill.

3. What have astronauts left behind on the Moon?
   A. A portable TV; B. Ninety-six bags of wee and
   poo; C. A set of keys; D. Eighteen space helmets.

4. How many stars are in the Milky Way?
   A. 300,000,000,000; B. 1; C. 150,000;
   D. Nobody knows.

5. What created crop circles in the United Kingdom?
    A. Aliens; B. Disgruntled farmers; C. A blowtorch and a pair of rubber gloves; D. A plank of wood, a rope and a baseball cap.

6. What colour is space?
    A. Black; B. Colourless; C. White; D. Greeny-bluey-purpley.

7. How many humans have walked on the Moon?
    A. Twelve; B. Zero; C. One; D. 142.

8. Who destroyed Isaac Newton's research?
    A. Marzipan the Monkey; B. Diamond the Dog; C. Edward the Elephant; D. Harry the Human.

9. What crime were the English able to get away with if there was a full moon?
    A. Burglary; B. Punching your teacher; C. Murder; D. Urinating in public.

10. What was the first living creature sent into space?
    A. Dog; B. Fly; C. Human; D. Dinosaur.

11. Why were the first astronauts afraid they might explode?
    A. Too much excitement; B. Zero gravity; C. Alien attack; D. Build-up of fart gas.

12. Why might you not want to be the first person to walk on Mars?
    A. No way back to Earth; B. The smell;
    C. The embarrassment if you tripped over your own feet; D. Dangerous Martians.

13. What is special about Moon dust?
    A. Sharp enough to cut through spacesuits;
    B. Smells like gunpowder; C. Causes space hay fever; D. All of the above.

14. What is Jake Garn famous for?
    A. First man to wee in space; B. Most sick person ever in space; C. First person to do a backflip in space; D. Tried to stow away inside a spaceship without anyone noticing.

15. What does SETI stand for?
    A. The society for extra-tough igloos; B. Solving everything this instant; C. The search for

extraterrestrial intelligence; D. Sometimes even teachers are idiots.

16. Why should humans have listened to Aristarchus the Mathematician in 250 BC?
    A. He knew the Sun was the centre of the solar system; B. He invented the TV; C. He correctly predicted that schools would be boring; D. He said that dinosaurs were a better species than humans.

17. How many presidents of the United States have claimed to have seen UFOs?
    A. Zero; B. Six; C. Two; D. All of them.

18. What happens to the human body in space?
    A. It grows by a couple of inches; B. It shakes uncontrollably; C. It swells up over time like a balloon; D. It turns orange.

19. What does space smell like?
    A. Carrots; B. Farts; C. Burned steak; D. Nothing.

20. What might be outside of our universe?
    A. Nothing; B. Another universe; C. An infinite number of other universes; D. Nobody knows.

HOW DO ASTRONAUTS WEE IN SPACE?

Answers

1.	C	8.	B	15.	C
2.	B	9.	C	16.	A
3.	B	10.	B	17.	C
4.	A	11.	D	18.	A
5.	D	12.	A	19.	C
6.	D	13.	D	20.	A, B, C
7.	A	14.	B		and D!

Also available in this series:

How Fast Can You Fart?

The wildest, weirdest, funniest, grossest, fastest, longest, brainiest and best facts about history, science, food geography, words, and much more!
ISBN: 978 1 78219 766 9
£5.99

Did Romans Really Wash Themselves in Wee?

The wackiest, wittiest, filthiest, foulest, oldest, wisest and best facts about history!
ISBN: 978 1 78219 915 1
£5.99

Do Turtles Really Breathe Out of Their Bums?

The funniest, grossest and most amazing facts about all kinds of favourite animals!
ISBN: 978 1 78219 774 4
£5.99

How Many Greeks Can You Fit Inside a Horse?

The wildest, weirdest, funniest, filthiest, foulest, wisest, grossest, brainiest and best facts about myths and legends!
ISBN: 978 1 78418 654 8
£5.99

Do Dinosaurs Make Good Pets?

The wackiest, wisest, grossest, brainiest, oldest and best facts about the prehistoric world!
ISBN 978 1 78418 652 4
£5.99